Sandak

First Families: The Madisons

C –
921
M y

31171

DATE DUE

1992

EMCO

PRINTED IN U.S.A.

The
Madisons

by
Cass R. Sandak

CRESTWOOD HOUSE
New York

Maxwell Macmillan Canada
Toronto

Maxwell Macmillan International
New York   Oxford   Singapore   Sydney

Library of Congress Cataloging-in-Publication Data
Sandak, Cass R.
   The Madisons / by Cass R. Sandak. — 1st ed.
      p.   cm. — (First families)
   Includes bibliographical references and index.
   Summary: A biography of the "Father of the Constitution," with special emphasis on the White House years
and James Madison's life with Dolley.
   ISBN 0-89686-642-4
   1. Madison, James, 1751–1836—Juvenile literature. 2. Madison, Dolley, 1768–1849—Juvenile literature. 3.
Presidents—United States—Biography—Juvenile literature. 4. Presidents—United States—Wives—Biography—
Juvenile literature. [1. Madison, James, 1751–1836. 2. Presidents. 3. Madison, Dolley, 1768–1849. 4. First ladies.]
I. Title. II. Series: Sandak, Cass R. First families.
E342.S26   1992
973.5'1'0922—dc20
[B]   92-14040

Photo Credits
Cover: The Bettmann Archive
The Bettmann Archive: 4, 7, 11, 12, 13, 15, 16, 19, 25, 26, 30, 34, 36, 37, 39, 40, 43
Thomas Gilcrease Institute of American History and Art: 20
Montpelier: 22

Macmillan Publishing Company
866 Third Avenue
New York, NY 10022

Maxwell Macmillan Canada, Inc.
1200 Eglinton Avenue East
Suite 200
Don Mills, Ontario M3C 3N1

CRESTWOOD HOUSE

Macmillan Publishing Company is part of the Maxwell Communication Group of Companies.

Produced by Flying Fish Studio

Printed in the United States of America

First edition

10 9 8 7 6 5 4 3 2 1

Contents

The White House on Fire

James Madison and his first lady, Dolley, were living in the White House during the last months of the War of 1812. By 1814, the battle was no longer being waged on distant seas. British troops had arrived in Washington, D.C., intent upon setting fire to every possible government building in the new nation's capital. The British troops were even talking about capturing the president and his wife. At the very least the British would set fire to the president's house.

Madison had gone to a battle site near Bladensburg, Maryland, just a few miles outside the city. As commander in chief, the president was needed there to support his troops.

Dolley remained behind. From the roof of the White House, she could make out the skirmish through her spyglass. She could also see the American troops begin their retreat. Courageously, Dolley wanted to stay until her husband returned. She delayed her departure from the White House until just minutes before the British troops arrived to set fire to it.

Dolley Madison saving the Declaration of Independence from the invading British

Rushing furiously from room to room, Mrs. Madison tried to save what possessions she could. Her first concerns were to safeguard the original drafts of the Declaration of Independence and the Constitution. These were kept at the White House.

But possibly Mrs. Madison's greatest achievement was supervising the removal of the famous Gilbert Stuart painting of the country's first president, George Washington. It was a full-length portrait that had been painted from life. This picture is the only White House furnishing that dates from the original house. It had been in place since 1800, when the John Adamses had it hung soon after moving in.

Because unscrewing the portrait from the wall would have taken too long, Mrs. Madison bravely ordered the ornate gilded frame broken and the canvas ripped from its stretchers.

Mrs. Madison probably did not actually touch the painting herself. It is likely that a servant did the real work. Whether Mrs. Madison did or not, the deed shows courage and foresight on her part, as well as a great sense of history.Whatever the truth, Mrs. Madison finally managed to escape and join her husband in nearby Virginia.

Then the British arrived. Before setting the house on fire, Admiral George Cockburn and his men toasted President Madison with wine from the presidential cellars. They ate the food that had been left out by servants who had speedily departed. The men also helped themselves to souvenirs from among the Madisons' belongings.

The burning of Washington by the British

Then the soldiers stacked up chairs and tables and set fire to them. In a very short time the house was engulfed in flames. A heavy rainstorm saved the house from total destruction. As it was, only the blackened outer walls remained standing.

Three years passed before people could live in the White House once more. By that time there was a new president, James Monroe.

Young Madison

James Madison was born on March 16, 1751, at Port Conway in King George County, Virginia. His parents were James and Nelly Conway Madison. Members of the Madison family had been in America since 1653. Madison's father was a planter and farmer, as members of the family had been for generations.

James was the oldest of 12 brothers and sisters, although five of them died when they were young. Soon after he was born, James was nicknamed Jemmy by his father. For many years close friends and family called him that.

Eager to learn as a youngster, James began to read books in his father's small library. When he was 11 James was sent away to a school on a plantation run by a Scotsman named Donald Robertson. James stayed with Robertson for five years, until 1767. While he was there Madison was instructed in logic, algebra, French, Latin and Greek.

When James was 16 he began two years of intense studies. This time he was tutored at home by Anglican clergyman Thomas Martin. The tutor was the person responsible for preparing Madison for college.

At 18 Madison was sent away to be educated at the College of New Jersey. The school later became Princeton University, one of the country's most prestigious schools. There were not many colleges in the colonies at that time. It was unusual that a Virginian like Madison would travel so far from home for an education.

During the two years Madison spent at Princeton he was a student of history. The spirit of patriotism was growing among the colonists. It was during this time that Madison first became interested in the issues of politics and government.

At Princeton in the late 1760s Madison and his fellow students were subject to strict discipline. This included long days of study that began at 5:00 A.M. There was little time for recreation. After only two years, in September 1771, James Madison graduated from college with a bachelor of arts degree. One of his classmates was Aaron Burr.

Madison had not really planned his future. So he stayed on at the school for most of an additional year to round out his education. It is probable that during this time he was considering becoming a minister in the Anglican church. While Madison remained at Princeton he studied Hebrew, philosophy, the history and government of ancient civilizations, as well as the principles of law.

As a student Madison had given some thought to a career in law. Between 1784 and 1786 he again considered preparing himself for the bar with a "course of reading."

Ultimately, he decided against it. He felt that his small stature, his weak voice and his lack of public-speaking skills would work against him.

Life in Virginia

Madison went home to Virginia after college. He continued studying theological topics with great seriousness. He also spent much of his time tutoring his younger brothers and sisters. It did not take Madison long to realize that tutoring was not particularly stimulating.

The Madison home was known as Montpelier. The main house at Montpelier had been built by Madison's father about 1760. The land had been passed down through the family from his great-grandfather, James Taylor II. Taylor had staked out a claim to more than 5,000 acres in 1716 as one of Governor Spotswood's Knights of the Golden Horseshoe. These men were among the first to explore the Virginia frontier.

In the autumn of 1774 Madison bought 200 acres of land from his father. That same year both Madisons—father and son—became members of the Orange County Committee of Safety. Madison's father was in charge of the militia.

In the spring of 1774 James took one of his younger brothers to school in New Jersey. During this trip James witnessed firsthand British mistreatment of the colonists. What James saw spurred him on. From that point on he felt the need to protest. He wanted to have a voice in the colonists' grievances.

When the war against England finally broke out in 1775, Madison had just turned 24. He was ready for service to the colonies as a member of the local militia. He drilled with his fellow militiamen but never saw active duty. An illness similar to epilepsy kept him from being sent into battle. In fact, Madison spent much of his life suffering from many minor ailments. He was never a strong person physically, although he lived to an advanced age.

In 1776 the young Madison was sent as a delegate to the Virginia convention. This group had been called to draft a state constitution. The next year he failed to be reelected to the convention. This was because he refused to ply the electors with rum and punch, as he was expected to do, according to the custom of the time. During this same period James Madison came to know and admire another Virginia patriot, Thomas Jefferson.

The Virginia convention

A Life of
Public Service

From 1776 to 1817, Madison worked almost continuously in positions of increasing importance. Madison served for four years as a member of the Second Continental Congress. When he was elected in 1779, he was its youngest member.

While Madison was working in Philadelphia in 1781, he met Kitty Floyd. She was a 16-year-old living with her parents. The young people liked one another and soon became engaged. Madison made plans to marry and take his bride back to Virginia and Montpelier. But just a few months later Kitty abruptly broke off the engagement and married someone else. The 32-year-old Madison was dejected and alone. As he often did, he buried himself in his work.

*Kitty Floyd,
James
Madison's
first love*

James Madison, the youngest member of the Continental Congress

In 1786 Madison served as a delegate to a meeting held in Annapolis, Maryland. This meeting, known as the Annapolis Convention, had been called by the Maryland legislature. It was the first acknowledgment that the new country faced problems that had to be worked out.

But only five of the thirteen states sent delegates. The delegates discussed problems with interstate commerce. They were also concerned with the states' conflicting claims to the extensive land holdings on the western frontier that had not yet been settled.

The Annapolis meeting was a failure, and it became clear that another convention would have to be held. The country needed a document setting forth a plan of government to find solutions to its problems.

Father of the Constitution

None of Madison's tasks was more significant than his participation in the drafting of this document—the Constitution of the United States.

The need for a constitution had become apparent between 1776 and 1787. After the revolution, the individual states began running themselves almost as separate countries. In the earliest years of independence, the war against England had provided a focus that unified the former colonies. Now the Articles of Confederation—the original plan of government adopted by the country—were not furnishing enough guidance for the young nation.

As a delegate from Virginia, Madison traveled to Philadelphia to the Constitutional Convention in May 1787. His idea was for a strong central government that would unite all the states while each kept its identity. The Constitutional Convention resulted in 86 days of continuous debate. On 71 of those days, Madison made impassioned speeches in defense of the document.

No other mind contributed so much to the Constitution. No other delegate to the convention was as well informed about the systems of government of nations around the world and throughout recorded history. Nor was anybody as well stocked with ideas for making the American government the fairest democracy ever created.

The Constitution was much more Madison's creation than he is often given credit for. Madison conceived the so-called Virginia Plan, designed to strengthen the ties of business and commerce between the states. Among the ideas that Madison's Virginia Plan outlined was the establishment of the office of the chief executive, or president. As well, he saw the need for an elaborate court system with a single Supreme Court for the nation. Madison also presented the idea of a single Congress with two houses. This was a compromise to satisfy people who wanted each state to have equal representation (the Senate) and those who believed representation should be based on population (the House of Representatives).

With some alterations it was Madison's plan that emerged from the Constitutional Convention as the Constitution of the United States. The document was signed first by George Washington on September 17, 1787. Then 39 more people added their names.

The signing of the Constitution

THE

FEDERALIST:

A COLLECTION

OF

ESSAYS,

WRITTEN IN FAVOUR OF THE

NEW CONSTITUTION,

AS AGREED UPON BY THE FEDERAL CONVENTION,
SEPTEMBER 17, 1787.

IN TWO VOLUMES.

VOL. I.

NEW-YORK:

PRINTED AND SOLD BY J. AND A. M'LEAN,
No. 41, HANOVER-SQUARE.
M,DCC,LXXXVIII.

The title page of the collected Federalist Papers

But that was only the beginning of the battle. Once the document had been created and signed, another intense period ensued. The plan of government needed to be ratified (or adopted) by representatives from each of the different states that made up the country.

During the months of debate Madison, along with John Jay and Alexander Hamilton, joined forces in writing the series of essays that became known as the Federalist Papers. The papers presented convincing arguments for adopting the Constitution. They remain one of the best commentaries on the document.

The Federalist Papers were first published in newspapers. They were later collected in book form under the title *The Federalist*.

Finally, on June 25, 1788, the Constitution was ratified. Madison's role at the Constitutional Convention made him a better-known figure than he had been before. From being a prominent Virginian he came to be a nationally known politician.

Madison was first elected to the House of Representatives in 1789. The House had been newly formed according to the Constitution's plan for the country's government. Madison served as a representative for a total of eight years. He quickly became a leader of Thomas Jefferson's political party, the Democratic-Republicans. Together Jefferson and Madison shared many of the same views about how the new country should be run.

Dolley

Dolley Payne was born on May 20, 1768, in a Quaker community that had been established in the Piedmont country of North Carolina. Her parents, John Payne and Mary Coles Payne, were both Quakers. They were natives of Virginia who had settled in North Carolina.

Dolley's upbringing was strict. The Quakers of her time were characterized by their serious natures and somber dress. But Dolley was a happy child known for her kindness, cheerfulness and high spirits. She had several brothers and sisters.

In 1790 Dolley married a lawyer named John Todd, Jr. Dolley had been poor until she met Todd. In 1793, after only three years of marriage, Todd died of yellow fever. The couple had two sons, John Payne and William. Young William died of yellow fever on the same day as his father. The sad mother and widow buried both husband and younger son at the same time.

Dolley's friend Aaron Burr introduced the young widow to the middle-aged congressman from Virginia. Philadelphia was still the young nation's capital when Mrs. Todd met the young politician. She described him as "the great little Madison" in a letter to a friend.

Madison was 43 and Dolley was 26. He was also an Episcopalian, a religious sect noted for its members' free enjoyment of the good things life has to offer.

Dolley Madison, known for her kindness and cheerfulness

It took several months of soul-searching by Dolley to reconcile her strict Quaker upbringing with marriage outside her faith. But Dolley shed her somber Quaker garments and sober ways of thinking. She seemed at last free to express the fullness of her personality.

By the time he was 43, most people viewed James Madison as a confirmed bachelor. Devoted to public service, he was intense, reserved and self-absorbed. But he was very much taken with the lovely young widow.

Because Madison was reserved and absorbed by work, most people thought he would remain a bachelor forever.

Upon the announcement of Dolley's engagement to Madison, then a member of Congress, Martha Washington advised her young friend, "Dolley, make this bachelor better known and more popular." George Washington was president at the time and his wife almost had the power of a queen. Her support could help make or break the career of any rising political figure.

Married Life

Dolley had only known James Madison for about a year when she married him on September 15, 1794, at a Virginia estate that belonged to Dolley's sister and brother-in-law. For a few years the Madisons continued to live in Philadelphia.

Dolley Payne Todd Madison was neither serious nor scholarly. She had had very little formal education, but she was able to further her husband's career with her charm. She introduced him to her countless friends. Dolley drew her husband out of himself and helped him mix with people who had the power to help him advance socially and politically.

James and Dolley Madison first went to live at Montpelier in 1797. Both of Madison's parents were still alive and continued to live in the house. Thomas Jefferson was a neighbor. His home, Monticello, was near Charlottesville, just 20 miles away.

Montpelier at the time Madison owned it

When Madison decided to expand Montpelier he consulted Jefferson. Jefferson's first suggestion was to make a broad classical portico. Jefferson even sent his own workmen to Madison to see that the job was properly done. Following the additions, the whole structure was coated with a thick limestone plaster and then painted.

Montpelier was not the same type of showplace as Thomas Jefferson's nearby Monticello. When James Madison inherited the estate in 1801, the house was still a two-story structure consisting only of two large rooms opening off two sides of a large hall that ran through the middle of the house. It was the same home that Madison had known as a child. This formed the central portion of the house, but James Madison had two large wings added at each end. Finally the house grew to be about 157 feet long and 33 feet wide. The Madisons had the first icehouse in Virginia—even before Thomas Jefferson had one.

The Madisons considered Montpelier their home, although government business called them away from the estate for long periods of time. Even after her children had grown up, James's mother continued to live there too. But, to make life simpler, she maintained a separate household in the south wing of the great home. She lived there until 1829, when she died at the age of 97.

A Rising Star in Politics

While serving in Congress, Madison saw the need for a Bill of Rights. Although the Constitution dealt with a great many issues, there were still some policies that needed to be made into law. By 1797, Madison felt that he was tired and wanted to return to Montpelier. He chose not to run for Congress again and he and Dolley went to live in Virginia. But politics again called and in 1799 Madison ran for—and easily won—a seat in the Virginia legislature.

Thomas Jefferson wanted to be the next president of the United States. Because Jefferson and Madison were as close in politics as they were in friendship, Madison worked hard to insure Jefferson's election to national office. Jefferson's rival, John Adams, was running for a second term. Thomas Jefferson became the new country's third president in 1801. Jefferson chose Madison to be his secretary of state.

Madison served in this post with distinction for both of Jefferson's four-year terms. As secretary of state, Madison worked closely with the president in handling problems as difficult as those faced by any secretary of state throughout our nation's history.

The Louisiana Purchase took place while Madison was Jefferson's secretary of state. Madison had a great deal to do with the negotiations that allowed the new United States to buy the huge tract of land from France. It was a purchase that would shape the westward expansion of the great country.

Thomas Jefferson was Madison's friend, neighbor and political ally.

Because Madison was such a capable and staunch supporter, it is not surprising that Jefferson backed Madison to succeed him as president of the United States.

In the autumn of 1808 Madison was elected president. He received 122 of the 176 electoral votes cast by electors from the 17 states that now made up the country. George Clinton of New York was elected to serve as Madison's vice president. Madison took the oath of office in 1809 when Thomas Jefferson stepped down.

The delightful Dolley Madison became the toast of Washington.

A Special First Lady

Thomas Jefferson had been a widower for almost 20 years before he became president in 1801 and went to live in the White House. He was the first president for whom the White House served as official residence throughout his whole term of office. John and Abigail Adams had lived in the barely completed White House for only a few months at the end of Adams's presidency.

Dolley Madison had been a fixture around the White House almost from the start of Jefferson's presidency. She served as first lady even before her husband was elected president. As wife of the secretary of state, she had served as official hostess for President Jefferson.

By the time that Thomas Jefferson became president, his two young daughters were married and had lives of their own. They generally lived away from Washington, but when they were at the White House with their father, Dolley Madison acted as mother to them. She guided them around Washington society and often accompanied them on shopping expeditions.

Mrs. Madison was also on hand when Jefferson's daughter, Patsy Randolph, gave birth to the first White House baby. Thus, the first child born in the White House was one of Thomas Jefferson's grandchildren. Jefferson's daughter named the child James Madison Randolph out of admiration for her father's friend and colleague.

First Lady—
Second Time

It was with great pleasure that Thomas Jefferson turned over the presidency to his close friend James Madison in 1809. Dolley now became first lady in her own right. She was 40 and at the height of her powers. Her husband was already 57.

The Madisons enjoyed the first-ever inaugural ball in Washington, held after the president was sworn in on March 4, 1809. It had been planned and hosted by a friend of the Madisons, Thomas Tingey, a government official who wanted to honor the first couple.

Dolley Madison quickly became the toast of Washington. Whatever James Madison lacked in charm, Dolley more than compensated for. She was kind to everyone. She was able to be tactful and polite in dealing with people— even those she did not especially like.

Dolley's charm lay not only in her pretty face, but in a kind and warm personality. A contemporary wrote that Mrs. Madison combined "all the elegance and polish of fashion" with "the unadulterated simplicity, frankness, warmth and friendliness of her native character."

Dolley is remembered for both the strength and gentleness of her personality. She was so well liked that her innocent foibles were often considered above reproach. Never has a first lady been so beloved and idolized as the perfect example of American womanhood.

In our own time, probably only Jackie Kennedy has come close to seizing the popular imagination with such force. But unlike Mrs. Kennedy, Dolley Madison continues to be a favorite historical figure for succeeding generations. Her popularity as a beloved first lady has never been and perhaps never will be exceeded.

Washington Society

When the Madisons had first come to Washington in 1801, the new city was still unfinished. But the lively couple contributed much to building up the social life of the brand-new capital.

The Madisons' dinners and receptions were both elegant and relaxed. They created the perfect atmosphere for advancing Madison's causes.

Because the couple had no children, the Madisons had more time and energy to devote to friends and other relations. Dolley's mother-in-law adored her.

The White House

The Madisons moved into the White House in 1809. The building was not even ten years old, but it still needed repairs and improvements.

Benjamin Latrobe, the architect, was engaged to supervise the work. Congress appropriated $12,000 so the repairs

The White House, after the British burned it

could be made. Another $14,000 was set aside to make necessary purchases for the household. Mrs. Madison oversaw the purchase of a piano and a china dinner service for state occasions.

Through James Monroe, the American minister in France, and his wife, Elizabeth, the Madisons were able to purchase a great deal of elegant French furniture. The furniture in large part had been the property of French aristocrats who had fled their country at the start of the Revolution of 1789.

For years Mrs. Monroe served as Dolley Madison's fashion consultant in Paris. She would buy trunkloads of gowns, turbans and yards of fabric and ship it all to Dolley Madison in the United States. Mrs. Madison was always able to dress in the height of European fashion, even though the Madisons never traveled abroad.

Before the White House was burned, the Madisons had proved to be a very welcoming couple at the mansion. Mrs. Madison's easy charm and relaxed manner gave her the reputation of a superb and friendly hostess. Often there were Wednesday-night receptions. These took place in what is now known as the Red Room. In the Madisons' time, however, the predominant color was yellow.

Washington Irving, one of America's noted authors, was a guest at one of the Madisons' Wednesday-evening "levees." He reported that "Mrs. Madison is a fine, portly, buxom dame who had a smile and a pleasant word for everybody." The president, however, failed to charm the man of letters. He was dismissed by Irving as "a withered little apple-John." Nor was Irving impressed with either Madison's stature or the dreary black clothes he wore as president of the United States.

In 1811 the Madisons hosted an elaborate Christmas party at the White House. Dolley sat at the head of the table in the State Dining Room. Dolley's sisters Anna and Lucy were present, as were many notable politicians. Washington Irving described Dolley and her sisters as "the Merry Wives of Windsor," after the spirited ladies in Shakespeare's play.

Mrs. Madison presided, and the party was a grand success. Festive roast stuffed turkey, chicken, goose and duck were served. All the food was put on the table at one time, including the vegetables and dessert. The waiters, who were mostly slaves, were paid 35 cents each for their evening's work, a generous amount for the time.

After supper, which lasted about an hour, the ladies and the gentlemen separated. The men smoked and did some serious drinking, while the women watched some light entertainment. Then they gathered together again, this time in what is now the Blue Room. By ten in the evening, the party was over and the guests began to depart.

In 1812 Mrs. Madison was responsible for the first wedding held in the White House. Her sister Lucy Payne Washington was a widow of one of George Washington's relatives. She was married to Thomas Todd, a Supreme Court justice who shared the same name as Dolley's first husband.

After the Fire

After the 1814 burning of the White House and other buildings in Washington, the building's original architect, James Hoban, was called in to supervise the restoration. By 1816 he had begun work on the executive mansion. This involved reconstructing the interior, strengthening the fire-weakened walls and covering the fire-stained outer walls with white paint.

During the reconstruction, the Madisons lived in other rented houses in Washington. There they continued to entertain and oversee the political and social life of the capital. Most of the time the Madisons lived in Octagon House, an elegant mansion not far from the burned-out White House.

The White House was restored just in time for the fifth president, James Monroe, to move in [to the reconstructed mansion] at the beginning of his term of office in 1817.

A Lady of Legend

Mrs. Madison was probably the earliest of the great first ladies, and certainly the first to become well known as a gracious hostess. Much of Washington jockeyed for invitations to her elegant entertainments.

No longer was Dolley Madison the sober Quaker girl. She was always dressed up in rich fabrics and elegant gowns. Even though she was tall, Dolley frequently wore great turbans, which added to her height. Sometimes these headdresses were decorated with feathers or jewels.

Madison said that being with Dolley was a delight. He loved to hear her stories about Washington life, and he especially liked the good humor she found in most incidents. But Mrs. Madison was more than just a delightful hostess. She was also a warm and caring person. Among her charitable acts was the founding of an orphanage in Washington, and she contributed to its upkeep.

Dolley had an exceptional gift for putting people at ease. She was not only able to make men feel at home, but she had a rare gift for making their wives comfortable as well. Women did not feel threatened by her or in competition with her. She was courteous to everyone and returned her social calls. Dolley always had a compliment, a kind word or something stimulating to say.

The Madison Years

During Madison's administration two new states were added. Louisiana (1812) and Indiana (1816) were admitted to the Union. Both were carved out of portions of the territory gained when President Thomas Jefferson and his secretary of state, James Madison, had negotiated the Louisiana Purchase from France in 1803.

Madison's years as president were marked by the deterioration of relations with Great Britain and France. The fledgling nation had not yet secured the respect of the older European powers, which still controlled the seas. As a result, captains of both British and French ships often seized American vessels and captured the sailors on those ships. Those sailors were sometimes forced to serve on British and French ships. The deeds amounted to piracy on the high seas, even though the perpetrators were the highly civilized nations of France and Great Britain.

Madison was an intelligent, cool-headed leader who did not believe in war—the same as Jefferson before him. However, both men conceded that war was sometimes necessary to protect a nation's interests. On June 1, 1812, Madison finally had to go before Congress to ask for a declaration of war.

Those who opposed Madison called the conflict "Mr. Madison's War." These were usually Federalists, and they were mostly New Englanders. Although Madison's popularity was at a low ebb, he was still able to gain reelection in 1812 for a second term.

Gilbert Stuart's portrait of James Madison

A drawing of British sailors seizing an American to serve in the British navy

Even though the War of 1812 ended in a standoff, Americans came to feel the war had been a success. This was largely because of the glamour surrounding General Andrew Jackson's victory at New Orleans in 1815. In fact, the Battle of New Orleans took place *after* the peace treaty officially ending the War of 1812 had been signed. Because of the length of time it took to get messages across the Atlantic, no one realized the war was actually over. The war was really a stalemate that ended only when the Treaty of Ghent was signed. But the victory at New Orleans meant something else to Americans. That battle was perceived as a victory. And the war resulted in an upsurge of national pride.

Americans viewed the Battle of New Orleans as a victory for their young country.

There was also a shift in American political thought: The influence of the Federalist party (mostly composed of intellectual New Englanders), which had opposed the war, was weakened and rejected by most of the country. As a result, the Federalist party disappeared.

Retirement

When the Madisons left the White House in 1817, they retired to Montpelier. After 1817 Madison emerged only once in an official capacity. In 1829 he served as a delegate to the Virginia Constitutional Convention. He also worked on several committees.

At Montpelier Madison's efforts at farming proved disappointing, and he could not get the estate to show a profit. Strangely enough, Madison's Virginia friends— James Monroe and Thomas Jefferson—also met with similar problems on their plantations.

Part of the problem was the burden and expense of handling the constant stream of guests who came by expecting to be fed and entertained. Sometimes the guests stayed for weeks.

The Madisons had an additional burden. Mrs. Madison's elder son by her first marriage, Payne Todd, had not turned out well. Both a drunkard and compulsive gambler, Payne had cost the Madisons heavily both in emotional stress and in untold sums of money.

James and Dolley Madison continued to entertain on a gracious scale. Madison still wanted to be included in the

James Madison, three years before his death

events going on around him. Even when he felt ill and was confined to bed, he had his bedroom door left open so that he could see and hear the gaiety in the hallway outside. In this way he could also make remarks as he saw fit.

Madison, Jefferson and Monroe all felt that the nation would not be secure unless its citizens were well educated. The three men served on the board of regents (the governing body) of the University of Virginia. In his will Madison left much of his considerable library to the university.

By the 1830s, one of the most disruptive forces in American political life had emerged. This was the states' rights movement. It threatened to shatter the ideal of a strong central government. After Madison's death in 1836, a note was found among his papers. In it he had written, "The advice nearest to my heart and deepest in my convictions is that the Union of the States be cherished and perpetuated."

When Madison died at the age of 85 on June 28, 1836, he was the last survivor of the Continental Congress and the last living signer of the Constitution. He was also the last survivor of the small group of men who took part in the nation's birth. These were the Founding Fathers, men who were responsible for setting up the United States and its government. Madison was a young man when the revolutionary war began and ended. Throughout his long life he served the country in many different capacities.

After her husband's death, Dolley found her income greatly reduced. Their lavish entertaining meant that most of their savings had been depleted.

After her husband's death, Dolley continued to be an important part of Washington life.

Even after selling the Montpelier estate Dolley still had trouble making ends meet. She moved to Washington, but after a short time there she was forced to mortgage her Lafayette Square house to raise cash. Neighbors, including Daniel Webster, often sent baskets of food in secret to her kitchen. In this way the former first lady had food but was spared the embarrassment of publicly receiving charity. As a result Mrs. Madison's dignity remained largely intact.

For years Dolley Madison was a distinguished member of Washington society. Whenever possible, subsequent presidents included the elderly but still sprightly woman in White House events. She acted as a matchmaker to Martin Van Buren's four bachelor sons. Indeed, one of her own cousins, Angelica Singleton, became the wife of one of Van Buren's sons. In the 1840s she was a guest at the marriage of William Tyler's daughter.

Dolley Madison's last official visit to the White House occurred early in 1848, when she was a guest at a ball given by President James Knox Polk. Later the same year she made her last public appearance when she attended the cornerstone ceremonies that marked the beginning of construction on the Washington Monument.

When Dolley Madison died on July 12, 1849, she was 81 years old. Even though she had been a widow for 13 years, she was still in the public eye. She was the last surviving link to the Founding Fathers of the United States.

James and Dolley Madison are buried side by side in two simple graves on the Montpelier estate.

The Madison Legacy

Standing only five feet six inches, Madison was the shortest president. But he had handsome features, a trim figure and a calm and dignified manner. His low voice was weak and he did not make a very good public speaker. But his speeches were well thought out and to the point.

James Madison, the father of the Constitution

Madison's vision was not the same as Jefferson's. Yet Madison was the more careful scholar and the one with the most common sense. He was the best read in history and political theory.

Dolley Madison's vivacity has often overshadowed her husband's presidential achievements. Madison was quick-witted and could equal his wife in charm and clever conversation. The burdens of public office, however, often detracted from the attention he could devote to social relationships.

Madison's greatest contribution to the country was in framing our system of government. It is true that he piloted the United States through a war with Great Britain and hostilities with France. But his genius is shown in his brilliant scheme of government, which is embodied in the Constitution.

James Madison inherited the presidency at a time when the country was just beginning to be divided over the issue of slavery. But Madison believed that the size and diversity of the country was what gave the United States its strength. So instrumental was Madison in shaping the plan of government that today he is usually remembered as the father of the Constitution.

For Further Reading

Anthony, Carl Sferrazza. *First Ladies: The Saga of the Presidents' Wives and Their Power, 1789–1961.* New York: William Morrow and Company, Inc., 1990.

Banfield, Susan. *James Madison: A First Book.* New York: Franklin Watts, 1986.

Clinton, Susan. *Encyclopedia of Presidents: James Madison.* Chicago: Childrens Press, 1986.

Desmond, Alice Curtis. *Glamorous Dolly Madison.* New York: Dodd Mead and Co., 1946.

Fisher, Leonard Everett. *The White House.* New York: Holiday House, 1989.

Friedel, Frank. *The Presidents of the United States of America.* Revised edition. Washington, D.C.: The White House Historical Association, 1989.

Fritz, Jean. *The Great Little Madison.* New York: G. P. Putnam's Sons, 1989.

Klapthor, Margaret Brown. *The First Ladies.* Revised edition. Washington, D.C.: The White House Historical Association, 1989.

Leavell, J. Perry, Jr. *World Leaders, Past and Present: James Madison.* New York: Chelsea House Publishers, 1988.

Lindsay, Rae. *The Presidents' First Ladies.* New York: Franklin Watts, 1989.

The Living White House. Revised edition. Washington, D.C.: The White House Historical Association, 1987.

Polikoff, Barbara G. *James Madison, 4th President of the United States.* Ada, Oklahoma: Garrett Educational Corporation, 1989.

St. George, Judith. *The White House: Cornerstone of a Nation.* New York: G. P. Putnam's Sons, 1990.

Taylor, Tim. *The Book of Presidents.* New York: Arno Press (A New York Times Company), 1972.

The White House. Washington, D.C.: The White House Historical Association, 1987.

Index